Camping Is the Best

by Elizabeth Franco • illustrated by Laura Zarrin

Lucy Calkins and Michael Rae-Grant, Series Editors

LETTER-SOUND CORRESPONDENCES
m, t, a, n, s, ss, p, i, d, g, o, c, k, ck, r, u, h, b, e

HIGH FREQUENCY WORDS
is, like, see, the, no, so, as, has, his, too, of, says

Camping Is the Best
Author: Elizabeth Franco
Series Editors: Lucy Calkins and Michael Rae-Grant

Heinemann
145 Maplewood Avenue, Suite 300
Portsmouth, NH 03801
www.heinemann.com

Copyright © 2023 Heinemann and The Reading and Writing Project Network, LLC

All rights reserved, including but not limited to the right to reproduce this book, or portions thereof, in any form or by any means whatsoever, without written permission from the publisher. For information on permission for reproductions or subsidiary rights licensing, please contact Heinemann at permissions@heinemann.com. Heinemann's authors have devoted their entire careers to developing the unique content in their works, and their written expression is protected by copyright law. We respectfully ask that you do not adapt, reuse, or copy anything on third-party (whether for-profit or not-for-profit) lesson-sharing websites.
—Heinemann Publishers

"Dedicated to Teachers" is a trademark of Greenwood Publishing Group, LLC.

Cataloging-in-Publication data is on file with the Library of Congress.

ISBN-13: 978-0-325-13806-0

Design and Production: Dinardo Design LLC, Carole Berg, and Rebecca Anderson

Editors: Anna Cockerille and Jennifer McKenna

Illustrations: Laura Zarrin; p. 32 Peter Bull Art Studio.

Manufacturing: Gerard Clancy

Printed in the United States of America on acid-free paper
2 3 4 5 6 7 8 9 10 MP 28 27 26 25 24 23 22
November 2022 Printing / PO# 34910

Contents

1. Dad Sets Up the Tent 1
2. A Treasure Map 13
3. At the Pond 23

Dad Sets Up the Tent

"I can set up the tent," Dad says.

Nick and Dad set up the mat.

Nick and Dad set up the sticks.

Nick and Dad set up the pegs.

The top is bent.

Dad is bent too!

Ack! The tent tips.

Nick and Dad get stuck and…

the back rips!

It is the end of the tent.

The tent is not set up.

Mom grins.

Mom rents a cabin.

The sun has set,
and Dad can rest.

2

A Treasure Map

Nick has a map.

The map has an X.

"Is it treasure?" Cass asks.

Nick nods.

Nick and Cass pass the cabin.

Nick and Cass pass the dock.

Nick and Cass hunt in the grass.

Stop! Nick can see a hint.

"X is on the rock!" Nick says.

It is a basket!

Mom and Dad hid it!

At the Pond

Nick sits at the pond.

A duck sets up a nest.

A big bug rests on a rock.

Nick can see a stem and a bud.

Nick dips his net in the pond.

"Ug!" says Nick.
"Rocks and mud!"

Nick sees steps in the mud.
"Is it a cub?"

No, it is not a cub…

Run!

Learn about...
A POND

Shhh! If you listen very closely, you can hear it: the quiet sounds of a pond. A *pond* is bigger than a puddle but smaller than a lake. Many plants and animals live near a pond. If you look on the *surface* of a pond—that's the top part of the water—you might see plants like water lilies and animals like turtles. You may even see a big, old bird like a heron!

If you look under the surface of a pond, you might see plants like algae and fish like minnows. You may even see a pond snail. These little snails glide along the bottom of a pond and eat up all the dirty gunk that no one else wants. That may sound gross, but it keeps the pond nice and clean.

Talk about...

Ask your reader some questions like...

- What happened in this book?
- What happened to Nick's tent?
- Do you think Nick had fun on his camping trip? What makes you think that?

- In this book, Nick sees all kinds of animals outside. He sees a duck, a bug, and even a skunk! *Pee-yew!* What kinds of animals have you seen outside?